STRANGERS ON OUR STREETS

Exploring the Faces, Challenges, and Hopes of Society's Hidden Populations, The Unseen Lives and Untold Stories

CHRIS LEO

STRANGERS ON OUR STREET

By Chris Leo

NOVEMBER 2024

Table Of Content

Introduction

Chapter 1
THE MANY FACES OF STRANGERS
The Diversity Among Us
A Call to See Beyond the Surface

Chapter 2
HOW DID THEY GET HERE?
The Consequence of Financial Hardship
The Weight of Mental Health Challenges
Escaping Abuse and Finding the Streets
Systemic Failures and Foster Care Aging Out
The Immigrant's Journey
Cycles and Systems Beyond Personal Control

Chapter 3
LIFE ON THE MARGINS
The Shelter Shuffle
Hunger and the Search for Sustenance
Health Without Healthcare
The Threat of Violence and the Need for Safety
Losing and Reclaiming Dignity
The Invisible Burden of Stigma
Survival and Resilience in the Face of Adversity

Meditation

"Give me your tired, your poor, your huddled masses yearning to breathe free, the wretched refuse of your teeming shore. Send these, the homeless, tempest-tost to me, i lift my lamp beside the golden door!" – Emma Lazarus, The New Colossus (inscription on Statue of Liberty)

Leviticus 19:33, 34

Introduction

We walk through the streets of our cities, towns, and neighborhoods, our minds preoccupied with lists of errands, calls to make, things to check off. In the midst of this hurried existence, we pass by countless people – some blending into the scenery, others just a blur. Among them are faces that stand out: the man on the corner holding a cardboard sign, the woman huddled under a worn blanket, the young person glancing nervously at passersby, as if hoping for someone to notice him yet afraid.

Every day, we encounter people whose lives run parallel to ours but who are invisible in plain sight. Their stories rarely make the headlines. Their voices go unheard. Yet behind every face lies a history and a journey, unique and profound. They are not statistics or objects of pity – they are individuals, each with dreams and aspirations once bright, now often dimmed by hardship but not erased. Whichever way, we must consider the people we pass by daily.

In cities across the world, there is a man named Carlos who once owned a small landscaping business. He was proud, hardworking, and dedicated to providing for his family. Yet, after a work accident left him injured, his savings dwindled fast. His family's financial security unraveled and he found himself navigating a system that offered little help. Carlos now lives in a shelter, still dreaming of the life he once had, longing to rebuild, to work with his hands again.

Then there is Dora, a young woman who left home at sixteen to escape an abusive household. For her, the streets provided an escape but also a new form of peril. She drifts between shelters and kind strangers' couches, attending night classes when she can, hoping for a way out. Her smile is quick, her laugh is soft, but her eyes carry a weight far beyond her years.

On the other hand, consider Tony, a veteran who served his country with pride, who fought in wars far from home. Now, he battles the effects of trauma and the isolating aftereffects of his experiences. The adjustment to civilian life has been brutal, and the support he was promised feels like a distant memory. Today, he wanders, haunted, a man who gave so much yet finds himself with so little.

In *Strangers on Our Streets*, we step into the lives of people like Carlos, Dora, and Tony – people we pass every day, often without a second glance. These are stories of resilience, of quiet suffering, and of humanity clinging to hope. This book invites you to slow down, to take a closer look at the people whose lives are mingled with ours in ways we may not see or understand. Each chapter will guide us through their experiences, their struggles, and the quiet strength they carry.

It is easy to sweep them up in our own lives, to feel the plight of others removed from our reality. Yet the truth is that every individual is part of a shared fabric, our stories linked by threads of hope, struggle, and dreams. *"Strangers on Our Streets"* is a call to see, to understand, and to act – not out of charity, but out of empathy. In reading their stories, we hope not to see them as strangers, but as part of our shared human journey.

Chris Leo

Chapter 1

THE MANY FACES OF STRANGERS

When we picture "the homeless," an image often comes to mind – a lone figure with weathered face, worn clothes, holding a sign at a busy intersection. However, this image is a simplification, a stereotype that misses the multipart, complicated reality of those we see on our streets. Each individual has a different story, a distinct path, and often, an unbreakable resilience that carries him or her through unimaginable hardship. This chapter peels back the layers, offering a glimpse into the diversity, humanity, and dignity of those we too often overlook.

1. The Elderly Woman with a Story Untold

Margaret is 73 years old, a grandmother who used to spend Sundays baking cookies and spoiling her grandchildren. Her hands are arthritic now, fingers curled from years of labor as a tailor, her eyesight dim from the countless hours she spent stitching hems and sewing collars to make a living. Once, she had a small apartment with lace curtains and pictures of her children on the walls. However, after a fall broke her hip and drained her savings, she could not keep up with rent, and she found herself sleeping in her car in a city parking lot.

Every night, Margaret reads an old, weathered Bible by the light of a streetlamp, finding comfort in the verses she memorized as a girl. *"The Lord is my shepherd and I shall not want", and "Even though I walk through the valley of the shadow of death, I shall fear no evil; for you are with me, your rod and staff comfort me".*

Her voice is warm, her spirit bright, even as she tries to keep her dignity intact. Despite the pain and cold, she clings to the memories of her family and faith, still hoping that one day her children might come to find her. For now, she spent her days blending in with crowds, hiding in plain sight – a woman with a life and a family she can only visit in memory.

2. The Young Man with the Gift of Art

Danny is 24, with a gift for drawing that could rival some of the most renowned street artists. His graffiti, colorful and full of life, has adorned alleyways and building walls, each piece a testament to his inner world. Once, he had dreams of becoming a graphic designer, imagining his artwork on album covers or displayed in galleries. But with no stable home and a family that abandoned him early on, survival became his focus, and his art became his solace.

At night, he sketches on scraps of cardboard or torn notebooks, his creations capturing glimpses of his childhood, the skyline of the city he calls home, and abstract shapes that represent the inner turmoil he has carried for so long. The streets are his canvas, and though some people considered him a "vandal", he knows the beauty he brings to corners others avoid. Danny's story is one of talent hidden from view, of creativity forced to adapt to an audience that may never know his name.

3. The Veteran Fighting a New Battle

Teddy, a former Marine, returned from deployment over a decade ago with a chest full of medals and a heart weighed down by memories of a war that never left him. For a while, he found work as a mechanic, his hands steady, and his demeanor calm. Nevertheless, the nightmares came soon after, then the isolation. His family could not understand, and friends stayed away as he struggled to find himself in a world that seemed strange and indifferent. Eventually, he lost his job, his family, and even his sense of belonging.

Now, Teddy spends his days alone, navigating city streets that seem to grow colder with each passing year. His body may be strong, but his heart feels worn, the pride he once held now buried beneath layers of sorrow. Strangers pass him by, unaware of the battles he fought, the sacrifices he made, the loneliness that wraps around him like a cloak. In his pockets, he keeps photos of his fellow soldiers, his only remaining link to the life he once lived.

4. The Mother and Child Escaping a Dark Past

Sadie and her seven-year-old daughter, Mira, are inseparable, holding hands as they navigate city shelters and unfamiliar streets. Mira's wide eyes take in everything around her, and Sadie knows she must keep a brave face for her daughter's sake. Just a year ago, they lived in a house with a garden where Mira would play, where Sadie would tuck her in at night with a story and a kiss. However, that life shattered in a single night, when Sadie fled an abusive partner with little more than the clothes on her back and Mira's stuffed bunny in her arms.

The street is no place for a child, and Sadie is painfully aware of the uncertainty that shadows their days. Yet every morning, she finds the strength to put one foot in front of the other, for Mira's sake. She braids Mira's hair, packs their meager belongings, and searches for any opportunity to find stability. To the world, she may be another face among many, but to Mira, she is a hero – a mother fighting for a better life.

5. The Refugee with a Dream Deferred

Ahmad was a teacher back in Syria, a man who believed that education could change the world. He loved his students, young minds eager to learn, to ask questions, to grow. However, when the bombs fell and his city reduced to rubble, he knew he had to flee. Now, he wanders the streets of a foreign land, unable to speak the language fluently, with no home, no work, and only memories of the life he left behind.

Ahmad carries a small journal filled with notes in Arabic, fragments of poems, and lines of wisdom he once shared with his students. He dreams of one day returning to a classroom, to a place where he can inspire young minds again. Until then, he moves through the city, an invisible teacher, a stranger in a strange land, carrying with him the hopes of a generation left behind.

The Diversity Among Us

These are just a few of the countless faces we pass each day, stories that often remain unspoken, lives reduced to labels like "homeless" or "stranger." Each individual carries a unique story, a blend of hardship and hope, courage and vulnerability. Some come from different countries, driven by conflict or poverty. Others are young people searching for a place in a world that seems to have little room for them. There are artists, veterans, teachers, mothers, and fathers – each united by circumstance, yet distinct in experience.

The homeless community is not a monolith. They are as diverse as the city's buildings, as complex as its traffic patterns, as rich in history and depth as any family. In a single day, you might encounter someone who, with the right support, could contribute greatly to society, someone who could be a neighbor, a friend, even a teacher.

A Call to See Beyond the Surface

In each face is a life lived, a story worth telling. This chapter introduces only a handful of individuals, but countless more await beyond the street corners, parks, and alleyways. As you journey through this book, may these faces become less of a passing blur and more of a lasting imprint, each a reminder of our shared humanity. Because in the end, the people we pass by are not strangers at all – they are fellow travelers, each of us carrying dreams, memories, and an indomitable will to survive.

Chapter 2

HOW DID THEY GET HERE?

The people we see on the streets are there for as many reasons as there are faces. To say someone is homeless, marginalized, or vulnerable only skims the surface of his or her reality. Each person has a distinct path that led him or her to the fringes of society, often due to a tangle of personal, social, and economic factors. In this chapter, we explore these diverse journeys, shedding light on how circumstances beyond one's control – financial hardship, trauma, systemic failure – can force people into situations they never imagined.

The Consequence of Financial Hardship

Kevin worked as an industrial electrician for nearly two decades. His job was physically demanding, but secured enough to support his wife and three children. Yet, when he suffered a back injury, his life took a swift, devastating turn. With medical bills piling up, Kevin depleted his savings, even selling cherished family possessions to cover expenses. Weeks turned into months, and Kevin found himself unable to work or afford his home.

Before he knew it, the bills outpaced his income, and they lost the house. Kevin and his family moved in with a relative, but the strain was too much, and soon forced them to find shelter. For Kevin, it was dreamlike; he had once been able to provide everything for his family, yet now, they stood in line at a food bank, waiting for essentials. The fall into homelessness was fast, steep, and merciless.

Kevin's story illustrates a reality many face: how quickly financial hardship can escalate, sending once-stable families into crisis. He is not alone. Many people experiencing homelessness held jobs, owned homes, and raised families – until an unexpected event left them vulnerable. Job loss, medical emergencies, and financial instability can be all it takes to push people beyond the point of recovery. Burden bearers become burdens themselves.

The Weight of Mental Health Challenges

Michelle, a bright young woman with a talent for writing, had her whole life ahead of her. But beneath the surface, she struggled with bipolar disorder, a condition that made her world oscillate between exhilarating highs and crushing lows. For a time, she managed to keep her life together, but when her condition worsened, the strain affected every part of her life. She lost her job, isolated herself from friends, and eventually got an eviction when she could not keep up with rent payments.

Without adequate support, Michelle fell through the cracks. Each shelter she visited had limited mental health services, and the appointments she made with clinics often came with waiting lists too long to be of immediate help. Today, she drifts between temporary shelters and lives a life marked by inconsistency and survival.

Mental illness is a factor that affects countless individuals on the streets. Despite the strides made in mental health awareness, many people with conditions like schizophrenia, bipolar disorder, or severe depression find themselves ostracized, misunderstood, and unsupported. Inadequate mental health services, combined with societal stigma, create a cycle that often leaves them in chronic homelessness.

Escaping Abuse and Finding the Streets

Abuse does not only occur in stranger situations; often, it originates within the home, where one should feel safest. Mary, a soft-spoken mother of two, knows this all too well. For years, she endured an abusive relationship, feeling trapped by fear and concern for her children's well-being. Finally, one winter night, she made the brave decision to escape with her kids. They left with only a suitcase and the clothes on their backs, taking refuge in a shelter.

Though the shelter gave them temporary respite, Mary struggled to find stable housing, as affordable, secure options were scarce. Her abuser's presence haunted her, limiting her options and making each move feel uncertain. Many women like Mary turn to the streets or emergency shelters as a last resort, simply to protect themselves and their children from abusive situations.

Domestic violence is one of the leading causes of homelessness among women and children. Survivors often face limited resources, barriers to housing, and a lack of social support, forcing them into homelessness even as they seek to escape abuse.

Systemic Failures and Foster Care Aging Out

James entered the foster care system at eight years old, bouncing between homes and group facilities until he turned eighteen. When he aged out of the system, he was expected to transition into independence, yet he lacked a support network or skills for self-sufficiency. Like so many foster care alumni, he found himself alone, without a stable place to live or a job to support him.

James tried to hold down work, but with limited education and experience, it was a struggle. Soon, he was sleeping in his car, unsure of where to turn or how to navigate a world that seemed indifferent to his struggle. Foster youth face overwhelming odds when they age out of care: without family support, many lack resources for housing, education, or employment.

For youth aging out of foster care, the road often leads to instability, especially without a community to rely on or mentors to guide them. Without support, many become vulnerable to homelessness, finding themselves on the streets shortly after leaving the system meant to protect them. Most of them end up as street scoundrels.

The Immigrant's Journey

Ali came to America with his family, fleeing war in their homeland, Sudan. A doctor in his country, he hoped to rebuild his life, but the complex process of revalidating his credentials and finding work made it nearly impossible to make ends meet. With limited English skills, little local support, and the stress of adjusting to a new country, Ali's family struggled to stay afloat. Despite his determination, he soon faced eviction, unable to pay rent.

For many immigrants, the barriers of language, employment, and legal status lead to a life on the margins. Their resilience is evident, but without opportunities to work legally, afford housing, or access support, they face impossible choices. For Ali, the dream of a better life became a harsh reality, one where his skills and dedication were met with bureaucratic red tape rather than opportunity.

Immigrants and refugees often come to new countries in search of hope and stability, yet they face unique hurdles that can lead to poverty and, ultimately, homelessness. Their stories highlight the way systemic barriers keep people marginalized, even when they arrive with valuable skills and a desire to contribute.

Cycles and Systems Beyond Personal Control

The paths that lead people to the streets are rarely linear or entirely personal. They involve a complex blend of factors, including systemic gaps that fail to support the vulnerable and unforeseen crises that can destabilize anyone's life. Whether the issue is lack of affordable housing, inadequate mental health resources, the loss of a job, or an abusive relationship, each of these factors reveals how our systems often fail those most in need.

The truth is, anyone can be one crisis away from homelessness. Forces that affect entire communities shape the paths that lead here. They make it clear that the issue is not individual failings but a collective responsibility. Homelessness is not a problem "they" face but a reality that speaks to the health of our societies and the policies that shape them.

In each of these stories lies a reminder that homelessness is not just a matter of personal choice or circumstance. It is a complex social issue, a consequence of systemic failures, and a call to address the underlying factors that lead people into lives of uncertainty. This chapter gives just a glimpse of the myriad ways people end up on the streets. It is an invitation to understand the diversity of their journeys and to see homelessness not as an isolated issue but as a pressing concern that deserves collective attention and compassionate action.

Chapter 3

LIFE ON THE MARGINS

Once someone reaches the streets, the challenges multiply. Basic needs – shelter, food, safety, and healthcare – are no longer guaranteed, and the effort to survive becomes an exhausting daily routine. Life on the margins of society is not only a struggle against external forces but also an internal battle to maintain one's dignity, hope, and sense of self.

In this chapter, we explore the daily realities of those living on the streets, focusing on the extraordinary resilience required to survive while also shining a light on the obstacles that perpetuate the cycle of homelessness.

The Shelter Shuffle

Each evening, the homeless in many cities line up in front of shelters, waiting for a chance to claim one of the few available beds. For people like Kevin, who lost everything after a work injury, the wait often begins in the late afternoon, hoping he will make it inside before capacity is reached. He stands, looking around at the crowd of faces he sees every day, people just like him, bound by a similar struggle.

Shelters offer a brief respite from the cold or the dangers of the streets, but they are often overcrowded, under-resourced, and, in some cases, unsafe. People are required to leave early each morning, taking their few belongings with them, only to repeat the cycle day after day. For those lucky enough to secure a bed, there is a short reprieve, but it is never permanent. The constant uncertainty can wear down the spirit, making each new day another hurdle in an endless maze.

Those who cannot get into a shelter face an even bleaker night; one spent seeking a safe corner, a hidden spot, or a warm grate. The lack of stable shelter is one of the harshest realities of life on the margins, where the temporary solutions become a way of life rather than a stepping stone to stability.

Hunger and the Search for Sustenance

Food is a daily worry for people like Mary and her young daughter, Mira. Living day to day without knowing where the next meal will come from makes it hard for Mary to think about anything beyond basic survival. Hunger dulls the mind, weakens the body, and makes it nearly impossible to plan for a future.

Food banks and soup kitchens offer critical support, but they come with challenges of their own. There are often long lines, limited hours, and not enough food to go around. For parents like Mary, there is an additional challenge: finding nutritious options for a growing child. For some, scavenging becomes part of the daily routine, leading them to convenience stores, public garbage cans, or fast food leftovers. This constant hunger strips away dignity and can push individuals into desperation.

Hunger is a quiet crisis within homelessness—a need that is constant and pressing. It robs people of energy, health, and ultimately the ability to break free from the streets. It is a simple need, yet so complex to meet when every day is spent just trying to survive.

Health Without Healthcare

For those experiencing homelessness, healthcare is a luxury rarely within reach. Illnesses go untreated, injuries fester, and chronic conditions are left unmanaged. Ali, the immigrant doctor who fled a war-torn country, is a perfect example of the irony in this crisis. He was once a healer, a caregiver, yet now he finds himself on the other side, unable to access the very services he once provided.

The healthcare system is often complex and prohibitive for homeless individuals, who may lack insurance, identification, or the means to pay for even basic treatments. Emergency rooms become the only option, yet they offer temporary fixes at best. Mental health services are even scarcer, and with long waiting lists and insufficient funding, they are often out of reach for individuals struggling with conditions like PTSD or severe depression.

The absence of adequate healthcare has consequences far beyond physical well-being. Illness exacerbates homelessness, making it harder to seek employment or maintain any form of stability. The healthcare crisis among the homeless is a silent epidemic, one that deepens suffering and cuts lives short.

The Threat of Violence and the Need for Safety

Life on the streets comes with constant exposure to danger, and for many, the fear of violence is a daily reality. Women like Michelle, who lives with bipolar disorder, find themselves vulnerable to assault, robbery, and exploitation. She moves through the city with caution, always mindful of her surroundings, always looking over her shoulder. The streets are unforgiving, and those on the margins are often left to fend for themselves.

Violence does not only come from strangers; it can occur within shelters, among others experiencing homelessness, and even from law enforcement. The need to stay alert, to defend oneself, and to find a safe place to sleep takes a mental toll, leaving people in a constant state of heightened stress. For women, children, and the elderly, the risk is even greater, and many choose hidden or isolated spots to avoid confrontations. Yet, this isolation can lead to greater vulnerability, creating a paradox where safety comes at the cost of even more isolation.

Safety is a basic human right, yet often a privilege people on the streets cannot afford. The constant exposure to risk and the lack of secure spaces turn daily survival into a series of calculated moves, decisions that can make the difference between life and death.

Losing and Reclaiming Dignity

One of the most significant losses people face on the streets is a loss of dignity. With no privacy, no personal space, and a constant dependence on charity, the sense of self-worth is eroded over time. Teddy, the veteran who once stood with pride in uniform, now struggles with the shame of asking for help. Each time he extends his hand for a dollar or waits in line for food, he feels his sense of self-worth slipping further away.

Homelessness often comes with judgment and stigma. Society's perception of the homeless person as "lazy" or "irresponsible" only adds to this burden, causing individuals to internalize these labels. This shame prevents many from seeking help, feeling unworthy of the support they need to survive. For people like Teddy, who served his country, this loss of dignity is particularly painful, as the values he once lived by seem distant and unreachable.

Yet, despite these challenges, there are moments where dignity is reclaimed, often through small acts of kindness and connection. A warm conversation, a shared meal, or a simple smile from a passerby can serve as a reminder of humanity. Many homeless individuals hold onto their dignity with fierce determination, refusing to let their circumstances define their self-worth.

The Invisible Burden of Stigma

Beyond the tangible struggles of food, shelter, and safety lies a burden, which is oppressive as well: the stigma attached to homelessness. People often see others experiencing homelessness through a lens of bias, judge them for their circumstances. This stigma creates invisible barriers, pushing them further into the margins and making it harder to reintegrate into society.

The social stigma isolates people emotionally, compounding feelings of shame and unworthiness. For James, who aged out of foster care, this stigma makes every encounter a challenge. Even well-meaning people can be unintentionally patronizing or dismissive, treating him as though he is somehow "less than" simply because he is without a home.

Stigma does not just affect how society views the homeless – it affects how they view themselves. Over time, this can lead to a sense of despair and alienation, eroding the will to reach out, seek help, or pursue change. Breaking the cycle of homelessness requires more than just resources; it requires a shift in how we see, understand, and engage with those on the margins.

Survival and Resilience in the Face of Adversity

Despite the overwhelming challenges, life on the margins is marked by extraordinary resilience. People like Mary, Ahmad, and Teddy find ways to carry on, to hold onto hope in the face of despair, and to keep moving forward, even if only one step at a time. Each day is a victory of spirit over circumstance, a testament to the strength it takes to endure.

For those who survive the streets, each day presents a fresh set of challenges, yet they persist. They navigate a world where each choice is a matter of survival, where resources are scarce, and where their worth is questioned by a society that often fails to see them as fully human. In this chapter, we see how resilience is not a choice but a necessity, a quality forged in the fires of adversity.

Nevertheless, resilience alone cannot and should not be the solution. Understanding the realities of life on the margins calls for empathy, and it demands action. The individuals in this chapter are not "problems" to be solved; they are people striving to reclaim their lives against all odds. As we recognize the resilience required to survive such hardships, we are also challenged to create systems that support, uplift, and provide pathways to a life beyond survival.

In the end, life on the margins is not about enduring hardship; it is about surviving with dignity and reclaiming humanity in a world that often looks the other way. The strength required to live this way is immense, and it should inspire us not only to see but also to act.

PART II:

SEARCHING FOR SOLUTIONS

In Part II, we turn our attention from the stark realities of life on the streets to the efforts made to address homelessness and marginalization. In a world that moves swiftly past the unseen and the ignored, these efforts are marked by innovation, resilience, and compassion. This section explores the people, organizations, and policies committed to creating meaningful change and highlight the pathways that bring individuals out of the margins and back into society.

Chapter 4

THE POWER OF COMMUNITY AND GRASSROOTS MOVEMENTS

In the face of widespread homelessness, communities across the world have stepped up to address the issue, launching grassroots initiatives aimed at offering practical solutions, support networks, and resources. These community-led efforts reveal a powerful truth: when people come together with a shared purpose, transformative change becomes possible.

This chapter will explore the individuals and organizations who have risen to the challenge, creating solutions that transcend the limitations of government systems, budget cuts, and bureaucratic red tape. From mobile clinics to community housing projects, these movements provide lifelines to those most in need, giving us a glimpse of what compassionate, people-centered care looks like.

The Human Impact of Small Acts

It often starts small. A few compassionate individuals notice a gap and decide to fill it, whether by distributing food, providing temporary shelter, or simply offering a listening ear. Consider Sarah, a retired nurse who began handing out meals in her neighborhood's downtown park after realizing the sheer number of homeless individuals in her area. Initially a personal effort, Sarah's gesture inspired friends and neighbors to join her, transforming her outreach into a weekly gathering where people come **not just for a meal, but also for connection.**

Such grassroots initiatives may seem modest, but their impact is significant. By creating safe spaces where individuals can find a meal, warm clothing, or a conversation, they also help to restore dignity and a sense of belonging. For many experiencing homelessness, these small acts of kindness remind them that they are valued. Sarah's story, like so many others, shows that sometimes the most profound changes start with the simplest gestures.

Safe Havens of Hope

In communities across the world, drop-in shelters and community centers have become crucial sanctuaries. These facilities offer more than just a temporary roof; they provide spaces for people to connect with services, form relationships, and even develop skills. For Mary and her daughter Mira, a local community center became a lifeline, offering food, clothing, and guidance to navigate housing applications and job searches.

Many drop-in centers now integrate a range of services under one roof: health check-ups, job training, and social workers who assist individuals in developing long-term plans. These centers also serve as places where people can shower, do laundry, and spend time in a safe environment away from the harsh conditions of the streets. The stability and support provided by these centers give individuals a foundation on which they can build.

In addition to immediate relief, community centers often play a pivotal role in helping people move from survival to self-sufficiency. Staffed by volunteers and funded by local donations, these centers show the power of communities to come together and support those in need, demonstrating that with the right resources, significant progress can be made.

Bringing Care to the Margins

Access to healthcare remains one of the most pressing challenges for homeless populations, yet grassroots initiatives have begun to bridge this gap in remarkable ways. Mobile health clinics, often housed in repurposed vans or buses, bring medical professionals directly to people on the streets. They provide essential services like health screenings, vaccinations, mental health support, and even dental care – services that are otherwise out of reach for many experiencing homelessness.

For Michelle, who has struggled with untreated bipolar disorder, one such mobile clinic provided a turning point. When a volunteer doctor offered her a consultation on the street, Danielle received her first formal diagnosis, along with medication and referrals for ongoing care. This simple encounter began her journey toward stability, underscoring the importance of accessible, community-based healthcare.

These mobile clinics represent a shift toward a more inclusive model of healthcare, one that recognizes the unique challenges faced by those on the streets. Funded by local donations, grants, and staffed largely by volunteers, these initiatives are a testament to what can happen when healthcare professionals work to make their services accessible to all. They remind us that healthcare is a human right and that the willingness to reach out to vulnerable populations can lead to powerful transformations.

A Radical Reimagining of Shelter

One of the most successful approaches to ending homelessness is the "Housing First" model, an initiative that flips traditional methods on their head by providing permanent housing as the initial step rather than the final goal. Under this approach, individuals are given a stable place to live before they are expected to address other issues like addiction, mental health, or unemployment.

In cities across the U.S., Canada, and Europe, Housing First programs have dramatically reduced chronic homelessness. By eliminating the requirement for individuals to be "housing-ready," the model removes one of the greatest barriers faced by homeless people: the instability that prevents them from securing employment, medical care, or a path forward.

James, a young man who aged out of foster care with no family or support, experienced homelessness for years. He describes the Housing First approach as "life-changing," explaining that the stability of having a home allowed him to pursue work, access therapy, and begin building a future. This model shows how essential housing is to any individual's sense of stability and self-worth.

Housing First initiatives recognize that without a stable foundation, all other interventions become secondary. A profound shift that challenges preconceived ideas about "deservingness" and "readiness," emphasizing that everyone deserves a safe place to live, without conditions or qualifiers.

The Role of Faith-Based Organizations

Faith-based organizations have long been on the front lines of helping the homeless, offering not only material support but also community and connection. Churches, mosques, synagogues, and temples often house food banks, run temporary shelters, and organize events that bring community members together to serve the homeless.

In Detroit, a coalition of faith leaders took their outreach a step further by building a tiny home village, a collection of small but comfortable homes offered to individuals facing homelessness. Each home provides not only a secure living space but also the opportunity for community, with shared gardens, resources, and regular gatherings. This initiative goes beyond temporary shelter, focusing instead on creating a space where people can rebuild their lives in a supportive environment.

Faith-based organizations, through their longstanding presence in communities and deep commitment to service, offer a unique type of support. They provide a sense of belonging and acceptance, treating individuals with respect and compassion. Their work highlights the role of spiritual and emotional support in recovery and reintegration, emphasizing the importance of connection alongside practical assistance.

Volunteers and Outreach Workers: The Unsung Heroes

Behind every initiative, program, or shelter is a team of dedicated individuals – volunteers and outreach workers who tirelessly serve those on the margins. They are the ones who walk city streets late at night, offering blankets, hygiene kits, and companionship to those without a home. They are also the social workers who follow up with individuals, helping them navigate complex systems, secure identification, and access essential services.

Volunteers like Jake, a former engineer who now dedicates his weekends to outreach, bring empathy and understanding that transcends official services. Jake describes his role as "being there, consistently," emphasizing that his presence alone creates trust. Through him, individuals experiencing homelessness know they have someone who cares, who sees them as individuals rather than as statistics.

Outreach workers often face emotional and physical challenges. They navigate difficult situations, witness immense suffering, and sometimes work within resource-limited environments. Yet their resilience and commitment to service remind us that homelessness is not only a societal issue but also a human one. Volunteers and outreach workers embody the values of compassion, empathy, and solidarity, reminding us that real change requires people willing to dedicate their time, hearts, and skills.

A Collective Effort for Real Change

The power of community and grassroots movements lies in their ability to reach people where they are and provide services in a way that is compassionate, inclusive, and respectful.

These efforts remind us that while structural change is essential, real progress is often achieved one life at a time, through the dedication of individuals who believe in the value of every person.

Grassroots initiatives do not just offer temporary fixes; they create lasting change by addressing the immediate needs of those experiencing homelessness while also tackling the systemic factors that contribute to the problem. By weaving together compassion, innovation, and practical support, these movements are a testament to what is possible when communities come together for a common purpose.

This chapter highlights the importance of community and the undeniable impact that ordinary people can make in the lives of others. While government policies and large organizations play essential roles, often these grassroots efforts bring true change to the people who need it most. In the stories of outreach workers, mobile clinic operators, and Housing

First advocates, we see the potential for a future where homelessness is not a forgotten issue but a shared responsibility.

With each act of compassion, we are reminded that homelessness is not an individual failure but a societal challenge that demands collective, empathetic solutions. The strength of these communities lies in their belief that every life matters, a conviction that can inspire us all to work toward a more just and inclusive society.

Chapter 5

POLICY AND SYSTEMIC CHANGE – REIMAGINING SUPPORT

While grassroots efforts address immediate needs, sustainable change in the fight against homelessness and marginalization requires systemic reform. The policies we create shape the social and economic landscapes that either prevent or perpetuate homelessness. In Chapter 5, we explore the policies and systemic approaches that are transforming how society approaches homelessness, examining both the successes and the ongoing challenges.

A History of Policy Gaps and the Rise of Modern Solutions

Historically, policies concerning homelessness have often been reactive rather than proactive.

Many early laws viewed homelessness as a crime, enforcing punitive measures instead of addressing root causes. These "vagrancy laws" criminalized poverty and pushed individuals into jails rather than providing avenues for support and recovery. Even as society's understanding of homelessness evolved, policies lagged, and the issue was largely relegated to local charities and nonprofit organizations.

It was not until the late 20th century that homelessness gained recognition as a complex social and economic issue requiring coordinated solutions. Governmental bodies, advocacy groups, and researchers began analyzing data and looking into systemic causes like affordable housing shortages, wage disparities, and mental health service gaps. This led to pioneering initiatives such as the McKinney-Vento Homeless Assistance Act in the United States, a landmark policy that provided federal funding for shelters, mental health services, and educational support for homeless children.

Today, as awareness around homelessness and systemic poverty increases, policies have started to reflect a more nuanced understanding of the issue. However, despite these strides, significant gaps remain, especially as challenges like housing affordability, job security, and healthcare access continue to impact society. The need for policies that not only provide immediate relief but also address these systemic barriers is more pressing than ever.

Affordable Housing and Rent Control: A Foundation for Stability

Affordable housing is widely recognized as a cornerstone of stability for individuals and families, yet it remains one of the most difficult issues to solve. In many urban areas, housing prices have skyrocketed due to factors like gentrification, real estate speculation, and the prioritization of luxury developments. For low-income households, this results in a cycle of instability, eviction, and, ultimately, homelessness.

Governments around the world are beginning to implement policies aimed at making housing accessible. Rent control measures, housing subsidies, and programs to build low-cost housing are among the most common strategies. In Finland, for instance, the government implemented a nationwide Housing First policy, prioritizing permanent housing for all, with impressive results. Finland's homelessness rates have decreased dramatically, and the model has inspired similar programs globally.

Still, housing policy remains contentious. Critics argue that over-regulation can deter investment in housing markets, while proponents highlight that without government intervention, the cycle of unaffordability will continue. Additionally, housing policy alone cannot solve homelessness; we must pair it with supportive services that address the unique needs of vulnerable populations, including mental health and substance abuse support. Affordable housing initiatives represent an essential starting point, but they are only one part of a much larger solution.

Addressing Income Inequality and Job Security

Income inequality has been rising for decades, with minimum wages failing to keep up with inflation in many countries. This has led to a growing number of "working homeless" individuals who hold jobs but cannot afford stable housing. For people like Lisa, a single mother of two who works two part-time jobs, low wages and irregular hours make it impossible to save for the future or afford even a modest apartment.

Increasing the minimum wage, expanding access to full-time jobs, and introducing paid family leave are policies that could significantly reduce the risk of homelessness. Many advocates argue that Universal Basic Income (UBI) could also offer a safety net, allowing individuals to meet basic needs without the constant pressure of economic instability. While pilot UBI programs have shown promise, implementation on a larger scale requires significant political will and funding.

Governments and companies are also exploring ways to support more secure work conditions, such as mandating that companies provide set hours or benefits to part-time and gig workers. Employment policies that ensure a living wage and job stability are vital to reducing the economic precarious that often precedes homelessness. By addressing these economic root causes, society can move closer to a future where fewer individuals and families find themselves on the streets.

Expanding Coverage for Vulnerable Populations

Healthcare policies are another crucial piece of the puzzle. Many people experiencing homelessness face untreated health conditions, whether physical or mental, that compound their difficulties in securing stable housing. Mental health disorders, substance abuse, and chronic illnesses are prevalent among the homeless population, yet access to healthcare remains inconsistent and often unattainable.

Universal healthcare is one approach that could dramatically improve the lives of homeless individuals, particularly in countries where medical bills can drive individuals into poverty or deepen existing financial instability. Countries like Canada and the UK, where healthcare is accessible to all, report lower rates of untreated illnesses among the homeless, though barriers like stigma and mental health resource shortages remain.

Expanding access to mental health services is especially urgent, as untreated mental illness is a significant factor in chronic homelessness. Some cities have introduced "street health" programs that bring medical services directly to those on the streets, an effective yet limited solution. For healthcare policies to be truly impactful, they must encompass preventive, acute, and ongoing care. These must ensure that we do not just treat people in emergencies, but also support in building long-term health and wellness.

Education and Job Training as Pathways Out

For many people, especially youth experiencing homelessness, education and job training are pathways out of poverty. However, homelessness itself often disrupts access to both. Children without stable housing frequently miss school or struggle to keep up academically, and adults experiencing homelessness face barriers to employment, from lack of stable addresses to limited skills.

Policymakers are beginning to recognize the importance of educational support for homeless youth. The McKinney-Vento Act, for instance, mandates that schools provide transportation for homeless children to ensure they can attend school consistently, and some states have expanded this provision to include school supplies and meal programs.

Job training programs for adults experiencing homelessness are also critical. Cities with vocational programs that provide skills training, apprenticeships, and job placement assistance have seen positive results, helping individuals transition from the streets to the workforce. By equipping individuals with skills and connecting them with employment opportunities, job-training initiatives give people the tools they need to build a more secure future.

Decriminalizing Homelessness

For many people experiencing homelessness, interactions with the criminal justice system are all too common. Cities often have laws that criminalize activities associated with homelessness, such as sleeping in public spaces, loitering, or panhandling. These laws perpetuate a cycle of punishment, where individuals accumulate fines or face jail time for behaviors that are largely a result of their circumstances.

Criminal justice reform advocates are pushing for an end to the criminalization of homelessness. They are emphasizing that **the world should not treat poverty as a crime**. Some cities have adopted a more rehabilitative approach, **offering individuals access to resources and programs rather than penalizing them.** For example, Seattle's Law Enforcement Assisted Diversion (LEAD) program redirects people arrested for minor offenses to community-based support services rather than jail, **helping individuals address the root causes of their behaviors.**

These reform efforts acknowledge that punitive measures only worsen homelessness by adding legal obstacles to securing housing and employment. By shifting the focus from punishment to support, cities can reduce homelessness rates and improve outcomes for individuals.

Public-Private Partnerships

Public-private partnerships (PPPs) are an innovative approach that brings together the resources of both government and private sectors to address homelessness. These collaborations can take many forms, from corporations sponsoring housing projects to healthcare providers offering free or discounted services to homeless populations. PPPs leverage private resources and expertise to supplement government efforts, often with greater efficiency and flexibility.

For example, in Los Angeles, a partnership between the city government and a coalition of tech companies resulted in an app that connects homeless individuals with available shelter beds, food resources, and other services. In other cities, real estate developers collaborate with municipalities to build affordable housing, combining private funds with public support.

PPPs have their challenges, including aligning profit motives with social goals, but when successful, they offer innovative and scalable solutions to homelessness. By fostering cooperation between sectors, PPPs represent a promising way forward, demonstrating that sustainable solutions are possible when society works together.

From Crisis to Commitment

As we explore policies that aim to reduce homelessness, we see that true progress requires not only funding but also a shift in societal attitudes. We should not view homelessness as an inevitable problem but as a challenge that we can address through commitment and collective responsibility. When governments prioritize affordable housing, healthcare, education, and supportive services, they pave the way for a future where homelessness is no longer a reality.

However, to realize this vision fully, policies must be adaptable and responsive to changing conditions. The stories of individuals who have benefited from these programs demonstrate that homelessness is not a fixed state. With the right support, people can and do overcome their circumstances.

This chapter emphasizes that while grassroots movements make an incredible impact, systemic change remains essential for lasting progress. The policies we advocate for and implement reflect our values as a society, and they have the power to either perpetuate suffering or create pathways to hope and resilience. By building a comprehensive and compassionate policy framework, we move closer to a future where no one has to call the streets their home.

Chapter 6

RETHINKING HOMELESSNESS SOLUTIONS

In recent years, new approaches to addressing homelessness have emerged that combine technology, community involvement, and fresh perspectives on housing and support. Chapter 6 explores some of these innovative strategies and examines how they are reshaping the landscape of homelessness intervention. These forward-thinking approaches challenge traditional methods, harnessing creative solutions to address the root causes of homelessness and provide sustainable pathways to stability.

Small Spaces, Big Impact

Tiny homes are gaining popularity as a low-cost, efficient solution to homelessness. Small in size but rich in potential, these units offer private, secure spaces at a fraction of the cost of traditional housing. For individuals who have spent years on the streets or in shelters, the autonomy and security of a tiny home can be life-changing.

Several cities across the U.S. and around the world have introduced tiny home communities specifically designed for homeless individuals and families. In Austin, Texas, the Community First Village provides a 27-acre tiny home community with services ranging from healthcare and job training to counseling and food support. This community model fosters a sense of belonging, helping residents reconnect with society and regain their sense of self-worth.

Tiny home initiatives emphasize that even modest living spaces can dramatically improve lives by offering stability, privacy, and dignity. By reducing the high costs and complex zoning challenges of traditional housing projects, tiny homes provide a practical and scalable solution that can be adapted to diverse locations and populations.

Smarter Support Systems (SSS)

Technology is transforming homelessness interventions by providing new ways to collect data, connect individuals with resources, and monitor the effectiveness of support programs. With smartphone applications, outreach workers can quickly track available shelter beds, identify food resources, and manage case information, allowing them to better assist people in need.

In Los Angeles, for example, a mobile app developed by the city in partnership with nonprofit organizations allows social workers to coordinate shelter availability in real-time, cutting down on the confusion and inefficiencies that have long plagued shelter systems. Similarly, cities like New York and Seattle use data analytics to identify areas with high homelessness rates, enabling them to deploy resources more effectively.

Moreover, some tech firms have developed platforms that allow for electronic storage of personal identification information. This is crucial for individuals who lose identification documents and face barriers in accessing housing, healthcare, and employment. With digital ID solutions, people can retain their information securely and recover it even if they lose their physical copies, streamlining their journey back to stability.

By integrating technology with human services, cities and organizations are reimagining homelessness support systems, using data to understand trends, allocate resources efficiently, and optimize support for those in need.

Healing Through Understanding

A significant number of people experiencing homelessness have endured trauma, whether from domestic violence, childhood abuse, or the hardships of street life itself. Recognizing the role of trauma is essential to effective support, as untreated trauma can influence an individual's ability to secure housing, maintain employment, and engage with social services.

Trauma-informed care is a holistic approach that emphasizes empathy, patience, and non-judgmental support. Programs based on trauma-informed care offer therapy, counseling, and peer support, creating environments where individuals feel safe and empowered. For example, in San Francisco, an organization called Covenant House offers trauma-informed housing programs tailored for young adults, many of whom have suffered abuse or neglect. By acknowledging past traumas and offering therapeutic support, Covenant House helps residents build confidence and develop resilience.

Trauma-informed care requires service providers to be trained in recognizing signs of trauma and in de-escalation techniques. This approach shifts the focus from simply addressing immediate needs to promoting long-term recovery and stability. By addressing the root causes of mental and emotional challenges, trauma-informed care gives people the tools they need to rebuild their lives with confidence and independence.

Empowering Through Employment

Employment plays a vital role in breaking the cycle of homelessness, yet many individuals face barriers such as limited skills, lack of experience, or gaps in their work history. Social enterprises, or businesses with a social mission, offer unique employment opportunities tailored to individuals who have experienced homelessness.

One such initiative, The Bread Project in Oakland, California, trains homeless and low-income individuals in culinary and baking skills, equipping them with a trade that is both marketable and meaningful. Upon completion of the program, local bakeries, cafes, and restaurants often hire graduates, providing them with a stable income and professional development.

In the UK, The Big Issue, a well-known social enterprise, gives homeless individuals a chance to earn money by selling a weekly magazine. The initiative not only provides a source of income but also fosters a sense of purpose, as vendors receive training, support, and even opportunities to transition to permanent employment. Social enterprises like The Big Issue serve as stepping stones, offering individuals the opportunity to build work experience, learn valuable skills, and move toward financial independence.

These social enterprises demonstrate that employment can be much more than a job; it can be a path to dignity, community, and long-term stability.

Housing as a Human Right

The growing movement to recognize housing as a fundamental human right is reshaping the way societies address homelessness. This approach advocates for legal protections and policies that guarantee access to housing, viewing shelter as a necessity rather than a privilege.

In Scotland, the government adopted legislation mandating that every citizen is entitled to housing, effectively criminalizing the denial of shelter. The country's Homelessness Act of 2003 obligates local authorities to provide housing to anyone at risk of homelessness. This model has led to lower homelessness rates and stands as an example of what is possible when we treat housing as a guaranteed right.

In the U.S., advocates are pushing for similar changes, with campaigns urging local governments to declare housing a human right and implement policies accordingly. Legal advocacy groups are fighting to remove barriers that prevent individuals from accessing housing, such as discriminatory practices against people with criminal records or poor credit histories.

Treating housing as a human right underscores that everyone deserves shelter and stability, setting the stage for policies that address homelessness in a fundamental, transformative way.

Ecovillage Models: Sustainable, Self-Sufficient Communities

Ecovillages are sustainable, self-sufficient communities that combine affordable housing with a commitment to environmental responsibility and communal living. These villages often include shared gardens, renewable energy sources, and communal kitchens, fostering both economic and social resilience.

In Portland, Oregon, the Agape Village has created an ecovillage for formerly homeless individuals, offering low-cost tiny homes, shared resources, and community activities. Residents work together to maintain the village, sharing chores and participating in workshops on topics like gardening, cooking, and budgeting. The model provides not only a home but also a sense of community, which is essential for individuals who have often been isolated by their experiences of homelessness.

Ecovillages present a unique solution that combines environmental sustainability with social impact. By reducing costs through shared resources and emphasizing cooperative living, ecovillages offer an innovative way to house and support individuals on their journey toward stability.

Addressing Invisible Homelessness

While we focus much attention on visible homelessness, the "hidden homeless" population – those who are couch surfing, living in cars, or temporarily staying with friends – also requires urgent support. Families with children, in particular, often experience hidden homelessness, and the impact on young lives is profound.

Programs that provide temporary financial assistance, hotel vouchers, or rapid re-housing services can be crucial for these individuals. For example, Family Promise is a U.S.-based organization that offers shelter, meals, and assistance to families experiencing homelessness, allowing parents to regain stability without exposing their children to the risks of street life. Family Promise's holistic approach ensures that families receive the resources they need to transition from temporary shelter to permanent housing.

Supporting hidden homeless populations requires policies that recognize the diversity of homelessness experiences and allocate resources to those whose situations may not be as immediately visible but are equally critical. By addressing invisible homelessness, communities can provide comprehensive support to all individuals in need.

A New Vision for a Compassionate Future

As this chapter highlights, the future of homelessness support is being shaped by innovations that embrace creativity, compassion, and inclusivity. From tiny homes to technology, social enterprises to ecovillages, these forward-thinking solutions demonstrate that homelessness is not a problem we cannot solve but one that we can address through a blend of traditional support and new, adaptable methods. Intractable

By focusing on housing as a right, integrating trauma-informed care, and utilizing technology, we can create a holistic approach to homelessness that respects the dignity and needs of each individual. These innovations challenge us to look beyond temporary fixes and reimagine what true support looks like.

The innovations detailed here represent both hope and a blueprint for a compassionate society. As these ideas continue to grow and evolve, they remind us that a future without homelessness is possible – and that each step we take toward that vision brings us closer to a world where we leave no one on the streets.

Chapter 7

VOICES UNHEARD – LEGAL AND SOCIAL OBSTACLES

Every community has voices that struggle to be heard – voices that carry the stories, struggles, and needs of those who find themselves marginalized. They face a maze of bureaucratic, legal, and social obstacles that stifle their opportunities and restrict access to vital resources and justice. In this chapter, we will explore how these barriers operate and affect marginalized populations, particularly those in our cities who feel like "strangers" among us.

Bureaucratic Barriers

1. Red Tape and Inefficiencies

Bureaucratic red tape is often seen as a series of formalities that ensure accountability, but for marginalized people, it can become a trap that restricts their ability to access essential resources. Consider the hours spent filling out forms, meeting arbitrary deadlines, or gathering documentation that they may not even possess. For many, especially those without stable housing or regular employment, navigating these requirements is overwhelming and sometimes impossible. Bureaucratic inefficiencies disproportionately affect those who most need public assistance, effectively placing resources just out of reach for those unable to "prove" they need them.

2. Identity and Documentation

For people experiencing homelessness, undocumented immigrants, and others on society's fringes, lacking an official identity document can be a barrier with severe consequences. Legal identification is often a prerequisite for obtaining housing, employment, healthcare, and social services. However, the process to secure documentation is complex and often requires resources that marginalized people simply do not have. Without identity, these individuals are rendered invisible to the system, unable to access basic rights and entitlements.

Legal Obstacles

1. The Cost of Legal Representation

In theory, justice should be blind, yet in reality, it often favors those with the resources to navigate the legal system. Legal fees, court costs, and other expenses create a financial barrier for marginalized individuals who need legal assistance. Many cannot afford skilled representation, which significantly affects their ability to seek justice or defend their rights. Even with public defenders available in criminal cases, civil issues – such as tenant rights, immigration status, or family law matters – often require private legal support. Without adequate representation, the scales of justice tip in favor of those with resources.

2. Criminalization of Poverty

Many cities have laws that criminalize behaviors associated with poverty, such as loitering, panhandling, and sleeping in public spaces. These laws turn everyday survival activities into punishable offenses, forcing marginalized individuals into cycles of fines, jail time, and legal records. These criminal records, in turn, restrict future opportunities for employment, housing, and education, reinforcing a cycle of marginalization. The justice system, rather than providing support, often becomes a punitive force in the lives of those who are already struggling to survive.

Social Barriers

1. Stereotyping and Stigma

Public perception plays a powerful role in creating and reinforcing social barriers. Many marginalized groups face stigma that stems from misconceptions, fear, or societal bias. This stigma manifests in social exclusion and discrimination, whether in hiring practices, access to housing, or even within public spaces. Marginalized individuals become "others" and treated as though they do not belong, deepening their sense of alienation and limiting their opportunities.

2. Social Isolation and Lack of Advocacy

Marginalized individuals often lack advocates to amplify their voices and champion their needs. The social fabric that offers support to many – family, community organizations, and social networks – is often frayed or missing for people on the outskirts of society. Without these connections, they face a profound sense of isolation, making it harder to advocate for themselves or find allies who can help them overcome legal and bureaucratic obstacles. Social isolation compounds the sense of being unseen and unheard, leaving many feeling truly like strangers in their own communities.

Solutions and Paths Forward

1. Reforms and Access to Justice

Advocacy groups and legal aid organizations play a crucial role in helping marginalized populations access justice, but more systemic change is needed. Policies that reduce bureaucracy, lower legal fees, and expand the availability of legal aid can make justice more accessible to those in need. We must push for reforms that simplify access to identification, streamline processes for public assistance, and make the legal system more navigable for everyone, regardless of socioeconomic status.

2. Building Community Support Systems

Establishing inclusive, supportive communities where everyone has a voice can help alleviate some of the social obstacles faced by marginalized individuals. Community centers, support groups, and advocacy organizations provide spaces for marginalized individuals to find connection, access resources, and receive the support they need. Building awareness and empathy within the broader community can also help reduce stigma and foster a society that embraces and uplifts everyone, not just those in the mainstream.

Advocacy for Policy Change

Policy changes at the local, state, and federal levels can help dismantle the structural barriers that hold marginalized individuals back. This includes revising laws that criminalize poverty-related behaviors, developing programs to provide documentation for those in need, and ensuring that social services are accessible to all. Long-term change requires a concerted effort to address the root causes of marginalization and create a society where everyone, regardless of their circumstances, has a chance to thrive.

This chapter aims to highlight the challenges faced by marginalized communities in accessing justice and resources, as well as propose solutions to begin addressing these systemic issues. By understanding the specific barriers they face, we can work towards building a society where no one feels like a stranger in their own streets.

Part III

RESILIENCE AND REDEMPTION – STORIES OF HOPE AND HUMANITY

Our world often feels fractured and challenging, resilience emerges as one of humanity's most remarkable qualities. Part III of this book shifts focus from the struggles and obstacles faced by marginalized individuals to the stories of survival, hope, and redemption that arise from these experiences. Here, we explore how people, even in the face of profound hardship, find ways to adapt, grow, and reach out to one another. These are stories of individuals who, despite being overlooked or sidelined by society, display incredible strength and endurance.

These pages are filled with narratives of quiet heroism, unexpected compassion, and the incredible capacity of the human spirit to rebuild. Whether through acts of kindness between strangers, the unwavering support of a small community, or the perseverance of those who refuse to be defined by their circumstances, this section highlights the resilience and generosity that flourish even on the harshest of streets.

The stories in this part of the book are reminders that, at our core, we share a common humanity. They invite us to look beyond labels, judgments, and appearances, to see each person's story with empathy and understanding. In the resilience of those who endure and the redemption of those who rise above, we find not only their hope but our own – proof that compassion and connection are possible even in a world that often feels divided.

Through these narratives, we invite readers to see beyond the challenges and embrace the possibility of transformation. In celebrating these lives, we bear witness to the power of hope and humanity to illuminate even the darkest corners of our streets.

Chapter 8

ACTS OF KINDNESS IN UNEXPECTED PLACES

Kindness has a unique way of appearing when it has needed most, often in the least likely places. On our city streets, amidst the struggles and challenges of those who feel like outsiders, there are moments of extraordinary compassion that reveal the best of humanity. This chapter shares inspiring stories of individuals – strangers, volunteers, activists, and everyday people – who go out of their way to extend a hand to those who feel invisible and forgotten.

The Stranger Who Stayed

One frigid winter night, a man named Luis, who had been living on the streets for years, was resting in a public park. Alone and unwell, he was used to people passing by without a second glance. However that night, a young woman named Maya, on her way home from work, noticed his distress. Instead of moving on, she sat beside him, listened to his story, and called for medical help. Not only did Maya ensure Luis received immediate care, but she continued to visit him in the hospital and later connected him with a community shelter. Maya's simple act of stopping to listen grew into a bond that gave Luis the support he needed to begin rebuilding his life.

Volunteers on a Mission

At the heart of many cities are volunteer groups that dedicate their time to serving marginalized communities. One such group, "The Night Angels," operates every weekend, providing food, blankets, and essential items to those on the streets. Their commitment goes beyond basic needs – they bring respect, care, and a sense of belonging to the people they serve. Through these encounters, they learn names, hear stories, and restore dignity to individuals often seen only as statistics. The Night Angels' compassion, powered by the simple goal of making people feel seen, has helped countless individuals feel a renewed sense of hope.

Activists Bringing Lasting Change

In neighborhoods often neglected by policy and public resources, local activists work tirelessly to improve conditions for the homeless population. Individuals like Jonathan, a former street resident himself, are on a mission to change lives. Jonathan advocates for affordable housing, mental health support, and addiction services, drawing on his own experiences to push for tangible change. His activism has not only led to new programs but has also inspired others to see people on the streets as individuals with stories worth listening. For Jonathan, kindness is not only immediate assistance; it is about creating a world where everyone has the opportunity to thrive.

The Barber Who Gives Back

Marco, a barber in the city, decided one day that he would start offering free haircuts to people experiencing homelessness. Every Sunday, he sets up a chair in the local park and spends hours giving haircuts to anyone who needs one. For Marco, this is more than a free service; it is a way to restore confidence and dignity to people who often feel overlooked. His clients walk away feeling refreshed, with a renewed sense of pride and self-worth. By giving back in his own way, Marco transforms his skill into an act of kindness that brings a little more brightness into the lives of others.

Community Comes Together

In one neighborhood, local businesses and residents came together to establish a community pantry and shower facility. What began as a small initiative to distribute food has grown into a space where people can come to feel supported and safe. Volunteers from all walks of life come to serve food, listen, and provide encouragement. Local schools, churches, and businesses donate supplies regularly, while residents stop by to offer whatever help they can. This collective effort reminds us that community is not just about proximity but about shared purpose and humanity. In this place, people feel seen, valued, and loved, restoring a sense of community for those who might otherwise feel isolated.

This chapter is a testament to the power of compassion, demonstrating how small acts of kindness can make a profound difference in the lives of others. The stories in this chapter highlight that kindness does not require grand gestures; often, it is in the unexpected, humble acts that the deepest connections are made. Through these stories, we reveal how compassion can transform both the giver and the receiver, weaving threads of hope and resilience into the fabric of our communities.

Chapter 9

RISING FROM THE ASHES – STORIES OF RECOVERY AND CHANGE

For those who have faced homelessness or poverty, incredible resilience, grit, and a fierce determination to rise above their circumstances marks the journey to reclaiming stability and self-worth. In this chapter, we look into the lives of individuals who have not only overcome immense challenges but have managed to rebuild, finding new purpose and a renewed sense of hope along the way.

These stories serve as powerful reminders of the human capacity for recovery and change. It also shows that we can transform even the most difficult of situations into pathways to growth and renewal. Let us look at these few samples:

From Homelessness to Helping Others

Carl's journey out of homelessness began in the most unlikely of places – a community kitchen where he went for a meal one cold winter night. There, she met a volunteer who saw her potential and offered her a small job. Over time, Carl's responsibilities grew, and with the steady work, he was able to secure housing and begin building a new life. Today, he is a full-time employee at the very shelter where he once sought refuge, providing support to those who find themselves in situations he knows all too well. Carl's story is one of transformation: from surviving on the streets to giving back to his community, he embodies hope for those still in the midst of their struggle.

Rediscovering Purpose Through Art

For James, a veteran who found himself homeless after returning from service, recovery came in the form of creativity. When a local art program for the homeless introduced him to painting, James discovered a way to express himself, process his trauma, and reconnect with his sense of purpose. Over time, his art gained recognition, and he began selling his work, earning enough to afford stable housing. Now, he runs art workshops for other homeless veterans, encouraging them to find solace and healing through creativity. James's journey is a testament to the power of self-expression and the importance of finding purpose, even in the darkest of times.

Education as a Path to Stability

For many, poverty becomes a cycle that feels impossible to escape, but for Mary, education provided a way out. After spending years in low-paying jobs and struggling to make ends meet, she enrolled in a community college program with the help of a scholarship for single parents. Juggling studies, work, and caring for her young child was far from easy, but she persevered. Today, she is a nurse, with a stable income and a renewed sense of independence.

Her story illustrates the profound impact that education can have, serving as a ladder out of poverty and a means to build a sustainable future.

Overcoming Addiction and Finding Purpose

For Damien, the battle with addiction was a central part of his experience with homelessness. His turning point came when he joined a rehabilitation program that focused not only on recovery but also on personal empowerment and job training. With the support of mentors and a structured plan, he completed the program and secured a job at a local nonprofit firm. Today, he is a peer counselor, helping others who are fighting addiction. Damien's journey from rock bottom to a life of purpose and service is a powerful reminder that **recovery is possible with the right support and a willingness to confront one's past**.

Rebuilding a Family and a Future

Angel and her two children found themselves without a home after her husband left, leaving them in dire financial straits. At first, they relied on shelters and the kindness of friends, but she was determined to create stability for her family. She connected with a program that helped single mothers with housing and job training, and, over time, she secured a stable job. Angel's story is one of perseverance, as she not only rebuilt her family's life but also became an advocate for other single mothers facing similar situations. Her strength and determination shine through, showing how resilience and community support can rebuild lives.

The individuals in this chapter are examples of what it means to rise truly from the ashes. They have faced challenges that many of us might never fully understand, yet through sheer determination, support systems, and often the help of strangers, they have managed to rebuild lives marked by purpose and fulfillment.

These stories offer powerful lessons in resilience and remind us of the importance of extending support to those around us. In each story, we see that recovery is not only possible – it can also serve as a foundation for transformation, inspiring others to reach beyond their circumstances and seek change. Rising from the Ashes shows us that the journey to healing is as much about courage as it is about compassion, proving that new beginnings can be born from even the toughest of trials.

Chapter 10

BUILDING BRIDGES

In a world increasingly divided by economic disparity, cultural differences, and social inequities, building bridges across these divides has become more vital than ever. Organizations, charities, NGOs, and social enterprises are stepping up to address pressing societal issues, alleviate hardship, and bring hope to individuals and communities. Their efforts span continents, addressing needs around the world, transforming lives and inspiring others to act.

Alleviating Hardship: A Lifeline for the Vulnerable

Poverty and hardship manifest in various forms - homelessness, food insecurity, lack of education, and limited access to healthcare.

Organizations like Feeding America in the United States have become lifelines, distributing millions of meals annually to individuals in need.

In Asia, the Smile Foundation in India focuses on empowering underprivileged children and youth through education, healthcare, and livelihood programs, breaking the cycle of poverty for future generations. Similarly, in Africa, ActionAid International combats food insecurity and advocates for women's rights, ensuring communities have the resources to build sustainable futures.

The Caribbean region sees impactful work by groups like Food For The Poor, which addresses hunger and provides housing, healthcare, and education in nations like Haiti and Jamaica. By directly addressing basic human needs, these organizations bring hope and stability to millions.

Breaking the Cycle of Poverty Through Education

Education is a powerful tool for breaking generational poverty. In Europe, organizations like Teach For All focus on providing quality education to children in underserved communities, emphasizing the role of teachers as change-makers.

In Africa, the African Leadership Academy equips young leaders with the skills to innovate and lead in their communities, fostering a culture of entrepreneurship and self-reliance. Asia's Room to Read initiative emphasizes literacy and gender equality in education, ensuring girls have the tools to escape systemic cycles of deprivation.

The United States also sees transformative work through programs like the Harlem Children's Zone, which combines education, community-building, and parenting workshops to uplift families from poverty. These initiatives demonstrate the profound role education plays in creating lasting change.

Fostering Community: Rebuilding Connections in a Fractured World

Social enterprises and charities often serve as the glue that binds fractured communities. In the United States, Habitat for Humanity rallies volunteers to construct homes, fostering a sense of belonging for families who have been marginalized.

In the Caribbean, organizations like Sandals Foundation work to enhance community infrastructure while preserving local culture and the environment. In Europe, Caritas provides services to immigrants and refugees, offering food, shelter, and legal assistance to those seeking a better life.

In Asia, the Asia Foundation focuses on governance and women's empowerment, while in Africa, grassroots organizations like Barefoot College empower rural women to become solar engineers, creating sustainable and united communities.

Measuring Impact: Stories of Hope and Transformation

The true measure of success for these organizations lies in the lives they change. A young woman in Rwanda, empowered by ActionAid's leadership programs, starts a cooperative that provides jobs for her village. A child in Haiti, supported by Food For The Poor, graduates from school and pursues a career in medicine.

In the United States, families once living on the streets now call a Habitat for Humanity house their home, symbolizing a fresh start. A rural school in Nepal, rebuilt with the help of Room to Read, produces students who become advocates for literacy in their communities.

From the bustling streets of New York to the remote villages of Sub-Saharan Africa, these organizations show what is possible when humanity comes together to build bridges.

The Call to Action: Joining Hands Across Borders

The efforts of charities, NGOs, and social enterprises are a reminder of our shared responsibility to care for one another. Their work invites us all to join the mission – whether through donations, volunteering, or spreading awareness.

As we continue to build bridges across cultures and continents, we take a collective step toward a more equitable and compassionate world, one where every person, regardless of geography or circumstance, has the opportunity to thrive.

Easy Ways to Access the Services of These NGOs

Many NGOs and social enterprises dedicate themselves to making their services accessible to those in need. Here are some straightforward ways individuals can connect with them:

Online Platforms and Websites

Most organizations maintain websites that provide detailed information about their services, application processes, and contact details. Examples include:

> ➢ Feeding America: Online food bank locators.
> ➢ Habitat for Humanity: Volunteer and housing application portals.

Mobile Applications

Some NGOs offer apps for streamlined access to their services. For instance:

> ➢ Room to Read: Literacy resources for students and teachers.
> ➢ ActionAid: Mobile alerts on aid distributions.

Local Offices and Community Centers

Many organizations have physical offices or partner with local community centers where individuals can directly inquire about services.

Hotlines and Helplines

NGOs like Food For The Poor and Caritas provide 24/7 helplines to offer immediate assistance or guidance on how to access resources.

Social Media Platforms

Many charities use platforms like Facebook, Twitter, and Instagram to share updates and respond to queries.

Collaboration with Local Governments

NGOs often work with local authorities to distribute aid. For example, Smile Foundation collaborates with schools and health clinics to reach vulnerable populations.

Referrals and Community Advocacy Groups

Community leaders and advocacy groups often connect individuals with NGOs that can meet their needs.

Partnerships with Religious Organizations

Churches, mosques, and temples frequently act as bridges to NGOs, helping those in need find the right resources.

Networking Events and Public Campaigns

Awareness drives, charity walks, and public outreach events provide opportunities to learn about available services and the ways to access them.

By utilizing these channels, individuals and families can tap quickly and efficiently into the resources offered by these impactful organizations.

Part IV

SHAPING A COMPASSIONATE FUTURE – WHAT CAN WE DO?

As we have journeyed through the lives, struggles, and triumphs of those who have been marginalized, one pressing question remains, 'What can we do? How can we contribute to a future where no one feels invisible, where compassion and support are woven into the fabric of our communities?' This section, "Shaping a Compassionate Future", turns to each of us, inviting us to be part of the solution.

Compassion can start with a simple, small act, but when practiced collectively, it becomes a force powerful enough to drive change. Whether through volunteering, advocacy, or daily interactions, each of us has the potential to make a real impact. This part of the book provides actionable steps, inspiring ideas, and practical ways to engage with the world around us. It challenges us to look beyond our own lives and imagine a society where we all play a role in building bridges, breaking cycles of hardship, and fostering communities of empathy and support.

Shaping a Compassionate Future offers more than ideas; it encourages a shift in perspective, urging us to recognize the shared humanity in everyone we encounter. Together, we can turn empathy into action, transforming our communities one step at a time. So let us explore the possibilities and discover how, by working together, we can build a future that includes, uplifts, and values every individual.

Chapter 11

BREAKING DOWN BARRIERS

One of the most effective ways to address homelessness and poverty is through policies, innovations, and advocacy that tackle the root causes of these issues. Breaking Down Barriers explores the ongoing efforts and forward-thinking initiatives aimed at creating sustainable, long-term solutions. From government policies to community-led housing projects, this chapter dives into the strategies that are reshaping our understanding of poverty and demonstrating that we can create lasting change through compassionate, systemic action.

Policy Changes for Affordable Housing

A key factor in reducing homelessness is addressing the lack of affordable housing. Progressive policies that support the development of low-cost housing options, rental assistance, and incentives for property owners to offer affordable units have made a substantial difference in many cities. Programs like Housing First, which prioritize placing people in stable homes before addressing other issues, have proven to reduce homelessness rates effectively. By ensuring that safe, affordable housing is available, these policies are breaking down barriers to stability and giving people the foundation they need to rebuild their lives.

Community-Led Housing Initiatives

Community-driven projects are proving to be game-changers in cities worldwide. These initiatives involve residents, local businesses, and organizations working together to create affordable housing. Tiny home villages and cooperative housing projects are innovative solutions that provide safe, dignified living spaces for those in need. In these communities, residents not only find housing but also a sense of belonging, as neighbors support one another and work collectively to maintain their shared spaces. By involving those directly affected by homelessness, community-led projects create more effective, empathetic solutions.

Social Programs for Financial Stability

A critical component of overcoming poverty is financial stability, and innovative social programs are helping people achieve it. Guaranteed income pilots, for example, provide low-income families with a stable source of monthly support, allowing them to meet basic needs and reduce stress. Similarly, financial literacy workshops, credit-building assistance, and matched savings programs empower individuals to take control of their finances and create sustainable paths out of poverty. These programs offer more than money – they provide skills and support, fostering financial resilience that extends well into the future.

Accessible Healthcare and Mental Health Services

Healthcare and mental health support are often out of reach for those living in poverty. Innovative models like community health clinics and mobile health units are closing this gap by bringing accessible, affordable care directly to underserved neighborhoods. Integrated mental health programs, including addiction counseling and trauma support, address essential aspects of wellbeing, helping individuals stabilize and recover. By removing financial and logistical barriers, these healthcare initiatives ensure that everyone has access to the care they need, regardless of their financial circumstances.

Employment and Job Training Programs

Breaking down the barriers to stable employment is a crucial step in addressing poverty. Programs that focus on job training, skill-building, and job placement are creating pathways for individuals to secure sustainable employment. Organizations like Work Ready Alliance offer tailored training programs in fields like technology, construction, and healthcare, preparing individuals for in-demand careers. By offering not only training but also job placement support and ongoing mentorship, these programs enable people to break the cycle of poverty and gain independence.

Education Initiatives for Future Generations

Education is one of the most powerful tools in reducing poverty, yet barriers to quality education remain significant in low-income areas. Programs like *Bridges to Learning* focus on providing scholarships, mentorship, and tutoring to students who would otherwise struggle to access educational resources. By supporting children and young adults from under-resourced communities, these initiatives lay a foundation for future success. Education does not just open doors – it offers a way to break the generational cycles of poverty that often entrap families.

Advocacy for Fair Wages and Labor Rights

Wages that fail to meet basic living costs are a major driver of poverty, making advocacy for fair wages and labor rights essential. Organizations pushing for a living wage rather than a minimum wage are leading the charge in reducing poverty among working individuals. Policy changes supporting fair wages, workplace protections, and benefits like paid sick leave and affordable childcare empower people to achieve financial stability. These measures not only protect individuals but also strengthen communities as a whole, creating environments where everyone has a fair chance at a stable and fulfilling life.

Public Awareness and Shifting Perspectives

Finally, breaking down barriers requires a shift in how we view and address poverty and homelessness. Advocacy campaigns and educational programs aim to reduce stigma, raise awareness, and encourage the public to see homelessness as a systemic issue rather than an individual failing. By fostering empathy and understanding, these efforts encourage people to support policies and programs that address root causes rather than symptoms. This shift in perspective paves the way for a more compassionate, inclusive society that meets everyone's needs.

Breaking Down Barriers explores the myriad ways that policies, community efforts, and advocacy are creating paths out of poverty and homelessness. These approaches demonstrate that addressing the issue requires more than temporary aid – it requires sustained, collective efforts to dismantle the barriers that keep people in cycles of hardship. As we witness the impact of these programs, we are reminded that by working together, we can build a society where everyone has the opportunity to thrive. Each initiative in this chapter is a stepping stone, a vital piece in building a more equitable future that leaves no one behind.

Chapter 12

SMALL STEPS, BIG IMPACTS

Often, when faced with the enormity of issues like homelessness and poverty, it is easy to feel that our individual actions cannot possibly make a difference. Yet, history and countless stories of change show us that every big transformation begins with small, consistent steps taken by individuals like you and me. Small Steps, Big Impacts dives into practical ways each of us can contribute to positive change, proving that even the simplest acts can create ripples of compassion and progress throughout our communities.

Whether it is volunteering, supporting local businesses, or casting an informed vote, there are countless ways to foster a more inclusive and supportive society. In this chapter, we explore a range of actions that do not require significant time or resources – only a willingness to care and take part.

Volunteering Your Time and Skills

Volunteering is one of the most direct ways to make a positive impact in your community. Local shelters, food banks, community kitchens, and outreach programs are often in need of hands-on help, whether serving meals, organizing donations, or offering administrative support. Beyond traditional roles, there are also ways to use specific skills such as tutoring, mentoring, or offering professional advice on topics like financial planning or career building. Volunteering not only benefits those you serve but can also be deeply rewarding, offering a connection to your community and a sense of purpose.

Supporting Local Businesses and Social Enterprises

Economic stability within a community often starts with small, local businesses and social enterprises. By choosing to support businesses that create local jobs and reinvest in the community, you contribute to a cycle of sustainable growth and economic empowerment. Many social enterprises also have charitable missions, such as employing individuals transitioning out of homelessness or donating a portion of profits to community programs. Every purchase from these businesses reinforces their mission, proving that where you spend your money can be a powerful tool for social change.

Voting with Compassion and Awareness

Responsible voting is one of the most impactful ways to influence policies that address homelessness, poverty, and inequality. Voting is not just about electing leaders; it is about supporting policies that align with values of equity and justice. By researching candidates and ballot measures, attending town halls, and asking questions, you can vote with greater awareness and encourage others to do the same. Support for initiatives like affordable housing, living wages, and healthcare access starts at the polls, where our collective choices shape the communities we live in.

Advocating for Policy Change

Advocacy goes beyond voting; it involves raising your voice and participating in the ongoing conversation about societal change. Whether through letter-writing campaigns, signing petitions, or attending rallies, you can join efforts to push for policies that reduce poverty, expand healthcare access, and protect workers' rights. Advocacy can happen locally, within your community, or on a larger scale. By reaching out to representatives, spreading awareness on social media, or joining organizations dedicated to social justice, you become part of a movement working toward systemic change.

Educating Yourself and Others

Compassionate action begins with understanding, and educating yourself about the causes of poverty and homelessness can transform how you approach these issues. Books, documentaries, articles, and community events can offer insights into the barriers faced by marginalized populations. By sharing what you learn with friends, family, or through social media, you help reduce stigma and shift perceptions. Knowledge is a powerful tool; by challenging stereotypes and dispelling myths, you foster a more empathetic, informed community.

Practicing Everyday Acts of Kindness

Sometimes, the simplest acts of kindness have the most profound effects. Whether it is offering a warm greeting, lending a listening ear, or helping someone carry groceries, these small gestures can make a person feel seen and valued. For individuals experiencing hardship, a single compassionate act can make all the difference in a day filled with struggle. Kindness does not require any grand gestures; it's about acknowledging each other's humanity and creating a sense of belonging in shared spaces.

Supporting Community-Led Projects

Many communities have grassroots projects aimed at addressing local needs, such as neighborhood gardens, community fridges, and free libraries. These initiatives often rely on community participation and benefit greatly from volunteers or small donations. By contributing your time or resources, you can help sustain these projects, which provide vital resources, foster connection, and bring people together. Supporting local projects also empowers community members to take charge of their neighborhoods, reinforcing a collective sense of ownership and pride.

Donating Thoughtfully

While monetary donations are always appreciated, donating thoughtfully can extend your impact even further. Consider giving directly to programs that focus on long-term solutions, like education, job training, and mental health services. You might also consider donating specific items in demand, such as hygiene products, clothing, or educational supplies. Some people set up monthly donations or gather friends to contribute collectively. Each small amount combines to create a substantial difference, proving that thoughtful giving goes a long way.

Encouraging Empathy in Young People

The seeds of a compassionate future are planted in the hearts of our youth. By teaching empathy and kindness to children and young people, we create a foundation for future generations who value inclusion and care for one another. Engage young people in conversations about homelessness and poverty, show them examples of kindness, and involve them in community activities when possible. By encouraging their natural empathy and answering their questions honestly, you help foster a new generation ready to address social challenges with compassion.

Small Steps, Big Impacts reminds us that each of us has the power to contribute to a kinder, more inclusive world. Through everyday choices, thoughtful actions, and a commitment to understanding and compassion, we can create significant change. Countless individual steps are the path to build a compassionate society. Each one adding to a journey that leads to a more just, caring, and connected future. As we take these small steps together, we prove that every effort, no matter how small, moves us closer to a world where everyone is valued, supported, and empowered to thrive.

Chapter 13

CULTIVATING EMPATHY AND UNDERSTANDING

Empathy is a powerful force that, when nurtured, can bridge divides, reduce stigma, and inspire meaningful action. In communities where poverty and homelessness are met with empathy and understanding rather than judgment, change becomes possible. Cultivating Empathy and Understanding delves into the transformative effects of embracing compassion, encouraging open conversations, and shifting perspectives about the realities faced by those living on society's margins.

Empathy is not just an abstract ideal but also an approach that encourages us to look deeper, to ask questions, and to acknowledge the humanity in every person. This chapter explores how developing empathy at both individual and community levels can create environments that uplift rather than exclude, fostering resilience, connection, and collective responsibility.

Seeing Beyond Stereotypes

One of the greatest barriers to empathy is the persistence of harmful stereotypes about homelessness and poverty. Misconceptions can fuel biases that dehumanize and marginalize those in need, creating further isolation. By seeking to understand the complexities behind these issues, we begin to see people as individuals rather than labels.

Recognizing that homelessness and poverty often result from systemic issues – such as lack of affordable housing, mental health challenges, or economic shifts – shifts the focus from blame to understanding. This new perspective fosters an empathetic approach, emphasizing shared humanity rather than differences.

Listening to Lived Experiences

Hearing directly from individuals who have experienced homelessness or poverty is one of the most effective ways to cultivate empathy. Storytelling initiatives, public forums, and support groups that give space to personal narratives can reveal the challenges, hopes, and resilience within these communities.

By listening without judgment, we allow ourselves to step into others' shoes and see the world from their perspectives. These firsthand stories deepen our empathy; challenging assumptions and helping us understand the emotional toll of homelessness while revealing the strength that so often goes unnoticed.

Breaking the Silence

For many, poverty and homelessness are uncomfortable topics, avoided in public discourse and personal conversations. Yet discussing these issues openly is essential for reducing stigma and building compassion. In workplaces, schools, and homes, creating a culture of open dialogue encourages understanding and helps dispel myths.

Community events, book clubs, and classroom discussions can all be spaces where people learn more about these issues, ask questions, and share perspectives. By bringing poverty and homelessness out of the shadows, we foster an environment where people feel encouraged to learn, support, and advocate for change.

Teaching Empathy in Schools

Empathy is a skill that we can develop from a young age, and schools play a pivotal role in fostering compassion among future generations. Programs that teach students about social issues, encourage volunteer work, and promote inclusion can cultivate a mindset of understanding.

Activities like community service, empathy-building exercises, and classroom discussions on poverty allow students to connect with real-world issues. By teaching young people to care about the well-being of others, schools can help build a generation that views empathy as a core value and is prepared to address these issues with compassion.

Media Literacy and Challenging Perceptions

The way homelessness and poverty are portrayed in the media has a significant influence on public perception. Unfortunately, these portrayals often reinforce stereotypes or oversimplify the issues. Cultivating empathy means being mindful of the information we consume and questioning narratives that reinforce stigma.

Media literacy empowers individuals to look critically at the sources they encounter, seeking out stories that provide a fuller, more nuanced picture. By actively choosing media that highlight the voices of those with lived experience and that explore systemic issues, we foster a more compassionate understanding of these challenges.

Fostering Connections in Everyday Life

Empathy often begins in the smallest of interactions. Simple gestures like acknowledging people on the street, offering a smile, or engaging in conversation with someone who may feel invisible can have a profound impact. These small acts recognize a person's humanity, offering dignity and respect in situations where people often feel ignored or judged. Communities that encourage these everyday interactions build a foundation of trust and understanding, creating spaces where everyone feels seen and valued.

Encouraging Compassionate Language

Language shapes our perceptions, and the words we use to discuss homelessness and poverty can either reinforce stigma or foster empathy.

Avoiding dehumanizing terms and instead using people-first language – such as "person experiencing homelessness" rather than "the homeless" – reminds us that people are more than their circumstances.

Compassionate language respects individuals' dignity and encourages others to see them as whole human beings with unique experiences. By choosing our words carefully, we contribute to a culture of empathy, helping to shift public perception toward a more understanding and supportive view.

Supporting Community Initiatives That Build Empathy

Organizations that offer programs in empathy-building, community dialogues, and cross-cultural exchange are vital for creating compassionate communities. Programs like Community Conversations, which bring together people from different backgrounds to discuss shared issues, break down social barriers and foster mutual respect. By supporting these initiatives, we help create environments where empathy thrives, inspiring community members to see themselves as part of a collective effort to uplift and support one another.

Cultivating Empathy and Understanding is about transforming the way we see each other, especially those facing hardship. Empathy opens doors to deeper connection, trust, and collaboration, encouraging us to take responsibility not just as individuals but also as members of a shared community. When we make a conscious effort to listen, understand, and stand together with those in need, we build a foundation of compassion that can uplift entire communities.

In a world where division often dominates, empathy reminds us that our shared humanity is our greatest strength. As we nurture understanding, we create spaces where people are valued not for what they have but for who they are, fostering communities grounded in acceptance, support, and love. This chapter urges us to take the next step, embracing empathy not just as a feeling but also as a transformative force that can reshape our communities and help build a more inclusive, compassionate future.

Conclusion

A SHARED HUMANITY

At the heart of every encounter with a stranger lies a simple truth: we are all bound by the shared experience of being human. Stripped of the labels that divide us – race, class, culture, or circumstance – we each carry the same fundamental desires: to be seen, to be valued, and to belong. Recognizing this truth is the first step toward bridging the divides that keep us apart.

To see a stranger not as an "other," but as a reflection of ourselves, is to embrace the essence of a shared humanity. It calls us to look beyond appearances and assumptions, to recognize the dignity inherent in every person, and to understand that each life is as complex, as precious, and as worthy as our own.

This perspective is not merely a moral ideal – it is a necessity. In a world increasingly interconnected yet deeply fragmented, our survival and progress depend on our ability to empathize, collaborate, and uplift one another.

As you step back into your daily life, let this book serve as a reminder: the people you encounter, whether on the streets or in distant lands, are not strangers but fellow travelers on this shared journey of existence. Look at them with eyes of compassion, speak to them with words of kindness, and act toward them with a spirit of solidarity.

In the end, building a more just, inclusive, and harmonious world begins with this truth: **WE ARE ONE**. It begins with you and me. Let us live as such.